S0-ARL-707

DATE DUE			

971
K

Kalman, Bobbie

Canada from A to Z

CENTER SCHOOL
MARION, INDIANA

01022  Bound to Stay Bound Books, Inc.

AlphaBasiCs

CANADA

from A to Z

Bobbie Kalman & Niki Walker

Crabtree Publishing Company

AlphaBasiCs

Created by Bobbie Kalman

To Dylan

Editor-in-Chief
Bobbie Kalman

Writing team
Bobbie Kalman
Niki Walker

Managing editor
Lynda Hale

Editor
John Crossingham

Computer design
Lynda Hale

**Production coordinator
and photo researcher**
Hannelore Sotzek

Illustrations
Barbara Bedell: page 27 (top);
Antoinette "Cookie" Bortolon:
page 20; Brenda Clark: page 30
(bottom); Bonna Rouse: covers
(leaf), pages 5, 13, 22

Special thanks to
R.C.M.P.; The Ontario Ministry of Economic Development, Trade & Tourism; Air Canada; National Ballet School; Ramona Gellel and students of Precious Blood School; students of Michael J. Brennan and Pine Grove Elementary Schools; YMCA Camp Wanakita; Gregory Gianopoulos; Paul Holder; Roberta Scott; Chris Miller, Jason Miller, and Mike Jacobs

Photographs and reproductions
Graig Abel: page 13; Air Canada: page 26 (top right); Archive Photos: pages 10 (top left), 11 (bottom); Charlottetown Festival: page 10 (bottom); Confederation Life Gallery of Canadian History: pages 8 (bottom), 17, 21 (bottom), 31; Marc Crabtree: front cover (bottom right), pages 7 (top right), 9 (all), 12 (top both), 15 (top right, bottom both), 18 (top right, bottom both), 26 (top left); The CRB Foundation Heritage Project/Claude Charlebois: pages 10 (top right), 16 (both), 28; Ken Faris: page 25 (bottom); The Image Bank: Kay Chernush, page 6 (top right) & D.C. Productions: page 7 (top left); Imperial Oil Ltd.: page 14 (top left); Bobbie Kalman: pages 5, 23; W. Lowry/Visual Contact: page 26 (bottom); Diane Payton Majumdar: pages 18 (top left), 19 (right); Bob Mansur: page 11 (top right); The Metropolitan Museum of Art, gift of Erving and Joyce Wolf, (1982.443.3) detail: page 27 (bottom); The Ontario Ministry of Economic Development, Trade & Tourism: pages 8 (top), 12 (bottom left), 21 (top); Magdalena Titian: pages 6 (bottom), 19 (top, bottom), 24 (top, middle, bottom right), 25 (top left); other images by Digital Stock & Eyewire, Inc.

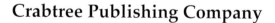

Crabtree Publishing Company

350 Fifth Avenue
Suite 3308
New York
N.Y. 10118

360 York Road, RR 4
Niagara-on-the-Lake
Ontario, Canada
L0S 1J0

73 Lime Walk
Headington
Oxford OX3 7AD
United Kingdom

Copyright © **1999 CRABTREE PUBLISHING COMPANY**.
All rights reserved. No part of this publication may be reproduced, stored in a retrieval system or be transmitted in any form or by any means, electronic, mechanical, photocopying, recording, or otherwise, without the prior written permission of Crabtree Publishing Company.

Cataloging in Publication Data

Kalman, Bobbie
  Canada from A to Z

(AlphaBasiCs)
Includes index.

ISBN 0-86505-381-2 (library bound) ISBN 0-86505-411-8 (pbk.)
This book is an alphabetical introduction to the history, geography, politics, culture, education, industries, and recreations of Canada.

1. Canada—Juvenile literature. 2. English language—Alphabet—Juvenile literature. [1. Canada. 2. Alphabet.] I. Walker, Niki. II. Title. III. Series: Kalman, Bobbie. AlphaBasiCs.

F1008.2.K34 1999   j971   LC 99-10788
                                        CIP

Contents

A is for **area**. In area, Canada is the second-largest country in the world. Russia is the largest. Canada occupies the northern half of North America and has the longest coastline of any country. It is surrounded by three oceans—the Atlantic, Pacific, and Arctic oceans. The United States is Canada's only land neighbor. Canada is made up of ten provinces and three territories.

Facts about Canada

Official languages: English and French
Capital City: Ottawa, Ontario
Population: 29 million
Currency: Canadian dollar (100 cents)
Area: 3,849,953 square miles
(9 970 610 square kilometers)

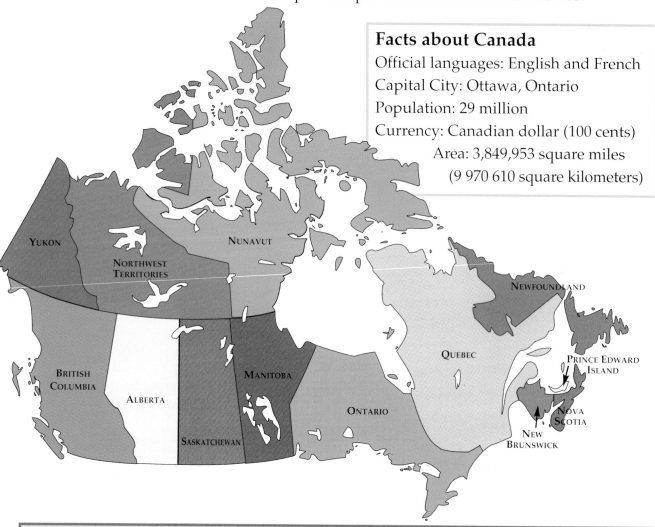

Provinces, Territories, and Capitals

BRITISH COLUMBIA	Victoria	NOVA SCOTIA	Halifax
ALBERTA	Edmonton	NEWFOUNDLAND	St. John's
SASKATCHEWAN	Regina	PRINCE EDWARD ISLAND	Charlottetown
MANITOBA	Winnipeg	**Territories:**	
ONTARIO	Toronto	YUKON	Whitehorse
QUEBEC	Quebec City	NUNAVUT	Iqaluit
NEW BRUNSWICK	Fredericton	NORTHWEST TERRITORIES	Yellowknife

is for **beaver**. The beaver is one of Canada's **national symbols**. A national symbol is used to represent a country. Canada's other symbols include the maple leaf and Canada's national police force, the **Royal Canadian Mounted Police** (RCMP). People around the world think of Canada when they see these things.

Much of Canada was explored and settled because of the beaver. In the 1600s and 1700s, hats made of beaver fur were popular in Europe. Hundreds of Europeans traveled to Canada to trade for furs and established settlements around the fur-trading posts. In 1975, the beaver officially became one of Canada's national symbols.

Early settlers had never seen maple trees before arriving in Canada. The maple tree became Canada's national tree in 1996.

In 1965, the Canadian government introduced the country's new flag, which has a maple leaf in its center.

The RCMP was formed in 1873 to maintain law and order in the Canadian West. It also kept the peace during the Klondike gold rush in the early 1900s. Today, RCMP officers, called Mounties, enforce laws dealing with drugs, weapons, and counterfeit money.

is for **cities**. Most Canadians live in cities. Canadian cities are clean and safe compared to those in many other countries. They offer hundreds of exciting things to see and do. Large cities are home to people from many different backgrounds. Major Canadian cities include Toronto, Montreal, Vancouver, Calgary, Ottawa, and Halifax.

(above) Montreal, Quebec, is Canada's second-largest city. After Paris, France, Montreal is the largest French-speaking city in the world! Its streets are crowded with cafes and fashionable clothing stores.

(above) Toronto, Ontario, is Canada's largest and busiest city. It is the center of business and banking in Canada. Toronto is also known for its CN Tower and Skydome, shown on the left side of this picture.

(right) Lunenburg, Nova Scotia, is one of Canada's largest fishing ports. The Fisheries Museum of the Atlantic is in Lunenburg. The town also hosts an annual fishing festival.

(left) Calgary, Alberta, is the center of the gas and oil business in Canada. This city is world-famous for its spectacular rodeo, the Calgary Stampede. The Stampede, which is held for ten days every year, is the world's largest outdoor rodeo.

(right) Vancouver, British Columbia, is located on the coast of the Pacific Ocean and is Canada's largest seaport. Its Stanley Park is the largest city park in North America. Vancouver enjoys Canada's mildest climate.

(left) Ottawa, Ontario, is the capital of Canada. It is located on the Rideau Canal. In summer, visitors and residents enjoy boating, fishing, and swimming in the canal. In winter, the canal freezes and becomes the longest outdoor skating rink in the world.

is for **dominion**. On July 1, 1867, Ontario, Quebec, Nova Scotia, and New Brunswick **confederated**, or united, to become a nation called the Dominion of Canada. A dominion is one of many lands under the rule of one government. Canada was part of the British Empire. Manitoba joined the Dominion in 1870. British Columbia became part of Canada in 1871, and Prince Edward Island joined in 1873. Alberta and Saskatchewan became Canadian provinces in 1905. Newfoundland was the last province to join. It became part of Canada in 1945.

(left) Canada Day, celebrated on July 1, marks the anniversary of Confederation. Across the nation, people celebrate with parades, concerts, barbecues, fireworks, historical displays, and other festivities. Canadian flags wave proudly from windows, doorways, and cars.

(below) These politicians and leaders are known as the Fathers of Confederation. Although some disagreed with the political ideas of others, they put aside their differences to make Canada a united country.

E is for **education**. Canada offers an excellent education to students from elementary school to university! Young Canadians attend school from Monday to Friday, September to June. In elementary school and high school they learn subjects such as language, math, science, history, art, and physical education. Most students finish high school around the age of eighteen. Many students then go on to study at one of Canada's many universities and colleges.

(left) Students can choose to attend a French or English school. Students in all schools, however, have classes in both languages.

*(bottom left) Canada also has many **parochial** schools, which students of a particular religion attend.*

(below) At the National Ballet School in Toronto, students spend half the day learning how to dance.

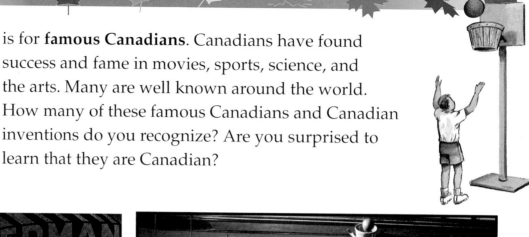

F is for **famous Canadians**. Canadians have found success and fame in movies, sports, science, and the arts. Many are well known around the world. How many of these famous Canadians and Canadian inventions do you recognize? Are you surprised to learn that they are Canadian?

(top left) A Canadian named Joe Shuster helped create Superman, one of America's favorite superheroes. (top right) Basketball was invented by a Canadian named James Naismith. It was first played with peach baskets. (bottom) Anne of Green Gables is a world-famous Canadian character.

(above) The West Edmonton Mall has over 800 stores as well as attractions such as an amusement park.
(left) The Canadarm is used on almost every space-shuttle mission.

(above) Superstar Celine Dion is from Quebec. She is one of the most popular female singers in the world, with fans in almost every country.

Did you know that...

- the Trans-Canada Highway is the longest paved road in the world
- Toronto's Yonge Street is the longest street in the world
- the CN Tower in Toronto is the tallest free-standing structure in the world
- more water rushes over Niagara Falls every second than over any other waterfall in the world (see page 23)
- the West Edmonton Mall is the biggest enclosed shopping center in the world
- the first chocolate bar was sold in Canada
- the first zipper was made in Canada

G is for **games** and **sports**. Games of all types are popular in Canada. People play board games, word games, and video games. In winter, sports such as skiing, snowboarding, curling, and skating are popular. Warm summer weather draws Canadians outdoors to enjoy sports such as baseball, tennis, soccer, football, sailing, swimming, cycling, and in-line skating.

(left) Canoes were first used by the Native peoples. Today canoeing is a popular sport.

(above) Canadians enjoy a wide variety of outdoor sports. Toronto's City Hall has a huge outdoor skating rink that thousands of people enjoy every winter. (top right) Children of all ages play baseball. Playing T-ball is a great way to learn the game. (right) Snowboarding is a popular sport on many Canadian ski hills. Hot dog!

H is for **hockey**. The first organized game of hockey was played in Montreal in 1873. Since then, hockey has become the most popular sport in Canada. Almost half a million young people participate in hockey leagues. Thousands more play hockey on frozen ponds, gymnasium floors, and on the street. Watching professional hockey is a favorite national pastime. The National Hockey League (NHL), which began in Montreal in 1905, was originally made up of only Canadian teams. Most NHL teams today are American, but many of the players are Canadian. How many famous Canadian hockey players can you name?

(above) Most people around the world think of hockey when they think of Canada, but hockey is not Canada's national sport. Canada's sport is lacrosse. Lacrosse was first played by Native Canadians and later adopted by European settlers. Lacrosse is played by two teams on a field, using a ball, two nets, and a lacrosse stick (shown right).

is for **industry**. An industry is a type of business that makes or sells goods or services. Canada has several major industries. Many, such as forestry, mining, and energy, make use of Canada's plentiful **natural resources**. Other industries include service, agriculture, and manufacturing.

(top left) Canada is rich in energy sources such as oil and natural gas. Canadians produce more energy than they use. Most of the extra energy is sold to the United States.

(top right) Canada is one of the world's largest producers of wheat, which is grown in the prairies. The grain is transported to other parts of Canada and the world.

(above) Canadians manufacture many types of goods, from cars to computers.

(right) Forestry is a large Canadian industry that produces lumber and paper.

is for **jobs**. Canadians work at thousands of different types of jobs to earn money. Many have jobs in Canada's major industries. Some Canadians, such as doctors, teachers, and fire fighters, are paid by the government. Others work for small businesses or are **self-employed**, which means they work for themselves.

*(top left) This business person is an **entrepreneur**. She runs her own business.*

(top right) These men work for a small construction company. They provide a service for homeowners.

(below) Medical workers include doctors, nurses, and emergency medical technicians.

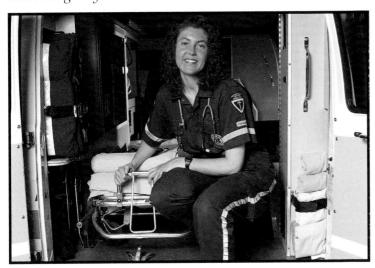

(above Police officers provide a service to the public. They patrol streets and help keep neighborhoods safe. Police officers are government employees.

K is for **kanata**. Many people believe Canada got its name from this word. Kanata is a Huron-Iroquois word meaning "village." In 1535, a French explorer named Jacques Cartier sailed along the St. Lawrence River and claimed all the land that he saw for France. According to a popular legend, he met a group of Iroquois on the shore of the river and asked them what they called their land. Pointing to their village, they replied "kanata." Cartier misunderstood the Iroquois and called all the land he claimed "Canada." The name did not become official until Confederation.

(right) Cartier and his men were the first Europeans to sail up the St. Lawrence River. They made three trips to Canada, searching for gold and other valuable resources.

(above) This is a reenactment of Cartier's first meeting with Native peoples along the St. Lawrence River. Cartier claimed the land for France. Many of France's important settlements, including the ones that became Montreal and Quebec City, started on the banks of this river.

is for **Loyalists**, or United Empire Loyalists. The Loyalists were the first large group of English-speaking settlers in Canada. In the late 1700s, the Loyalists moved from the thirteen colonies, which became the United States, to land that is now part of Canada. At that time, the thirteen colonies were fighting the War of Independence with England. The Loyalists wanted to remain subjects of the king of England, so they moved north to the British colonies of Nova Scotia and Quebec. This area included the land that is now the province of Ontario.

The Loyalists had to leave behind their homes, businesses, and most of their belongings when they fled the thirteen colonies. When they arrived in the British colonies, the king of England rewarded their loyalty with land, tools, and money.

M is for **multiculturalism**. Multicultural means "of many cultures." Canada is one of the most multicultural countries in the world. Its people have come from a variety of national and ethnic backgrounds. Some are Native Canadian; some are European; others are African, Middle Eastern, Caribbean, Asian, or Central or South American. Each group celebrates the customs and traditions of their homeland and also shares in the cultural celebrations of other Canadians. Every year, hundreds of festivals offer Canadians the chance to learn about other cultures as they enjoy the foods, music, artwork, and dancing of people from different ethnic backgrounds.

(top left) These classmates come from different cultures.
(top right) One of Canada's famous festivals is Caribana, which celebrates the cultures of the Caribbean Islands.
(below) Canada is a peaceful country because Canadians respect one another's differences.

(above) People from the same ethnic background often live and shop in one neighborhood, such as Chinatown.

N is for **Native Canadians**. The people of the First Nations and the Inuit are Native Canadians. They are also called **aboriginal** people because they are the descendants of the **original**, or first, peoples to live in Canada. Scientists believe that groups of people arrived in Canada from Asia between 10,000 and 30,000 years ago. Over thousands of years, the different groups, or **nations**, settled in different areas. The First Nations lived throughout the plains and forests of southern Canada. The Inuit settled in the Arctic. Each group developed its own language, religious beliefs, and culture, but they all shared a respect for nature. The Métis are also considered Native Canadians. They have both European and Native Canadian ancestors.

(above) These four Inuit friends are enjoying their recess break at school.

(below) An Inuit mother carries her baby in a pouch that is part of her coat.

*(above) This aboriginal grandfather and granddaughter are dressed in dancing **regalia**, or outfits. They take part in celebrations called **powwows**, which feature games, crafts, art, music, and dancing. Competitions are held, and prizes are awarded for the best dancers.*

O is for **O Canada**! O Canada is Canada's **national anthem**. A national anthem is a country's official song. People sing their national anthem to celebrate their country and show that they are proud. O Canada was first sung in 1880. It was a French song called *Chant Nationale* or National Song. Since 1880, the lyrics have changed several times. O Canada became Canada's anthem on July 1, 1980.

O Canada!
Our home and native land!
True patriot love in all thy
sons command.
With glowing hearts we see thee rise,
The True North strong and free!
From far and wide, O Canada,
We stand on guard for thee.
God keep our land glorious and free!
O Canada, we stand on guard
for thee!
O Canada, we stand on guard
for thee!

O Canada!
Terre de nos aïeux,
Ton front est ceint de fleurons
glorieux!
Car ton bras sait porter l'épée,
Il sait porter la croix!
Ton histoire est une épopée
Des plus brillants exploits,
Et ta valeur,
de foi trempée,
Protégera nos foyers et nos droits,
Protégera nos foyers et
nos droits.

Chant Nationale was written by two people from Quebec—Calixa Lavallée wrote the music, and Adolphe-Basile Routhier wrote the words. Few English-speaking Canadians knew of the song until the 1900s. In 1908, a school teacher from Toronto named Robert Stanley Weir wrote English words for the song, calling it "O Canada." Although politicians have made some small changes over the years, most of Weir's words are used in the English version sung today.

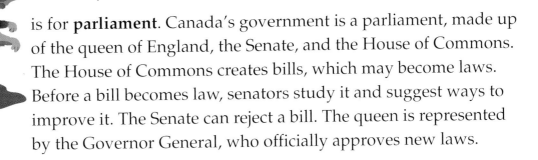

P is for **parliament**. Canada's government is a parliament, made up of the queen of England, the Senate, and the House of Commons. The House of Commons creates bills, which may become laws. Before a bill becomes law, senators study it and suggest ways to improve it. The Senate can reject a bill. The queen is represented by the Governor General, who officially approves new laws.

(right) The federal government's headquarters are on Parliament Hill in Ottawa, Ontario.

*(above) Canadians elect Members of Parliament (MPs) to represent them in the House of Commons, which is where laws are created. The MPs belong to different political parties. Each party is a group with different ideas about how the country should be run. The party with the most MPs forms the government. The leader of this party is the **Prime Minister**, who is also the leader of Canada. This painting shows the Canadian Prime Ministers who led the country from Confederation to 1968.*

Q is for **Quebec**. Quebec is Canada's largest province. It is called *la belle province*, which is French for "the beautiful province." In 1608, the first permanent French settlement in Canada, called New France, was established in Quebec. Today, the province is home to most of Canada's **francophones**, or French-speaking people. Many of Quebec's newspapers, television programs, radio broadcasts, and street signs are in French. The *fleur-de-lis*, shown right, is Quebec's symbol.

*(above) In 1608, a French explorer named Samuel de Champlain founded the settlement that became Quebec City, which is Quebec's capital. Today, Quebec City is the oldest city in North America. It is also the only **citadel**, or walled city, on the continent.*

Q is also for **quiz**. How much do you know about Canada's land and people? Take this quiz to find out. If you need help, flip through the book and you will find the answers.

- What is Canada's capital?
- What is the title of Canada's leader?
- What is the name of Canada's northernmost landscape? In which region is it found?
- In which region will you find endless fields of wheat and other grains?
- Name the region where you will find Canada's tallest mountains as well as its only rain forest.
- In which province do most French-speaking Canadians live?
- Which Canadian city is the oldest in North America?
- What is the name of Canada's largest city?
- Name two of Canada's national symbols.
- Name five famous Canadians or Canadian creations.

Every second, more water flows over this waterfall than any other. In fact, its name comes from a Native Canadian word that means "thundering water." What is the name of this waterfall?

R is for **regions**. Canada has six natural regions, shown on the map. They are the Arctic, Western Cordillera, Great Plains, Canadian Shield, Great Lakes/St. Lawrence Lowlands, and Appalachian Region.

Regions of Canada

- Western Cordillera
- Great Plains
- Precambrian Shield
- Arctic Tundra and Islands
- Great Lakes— St. Lawrence Lowlands
- Appalachians

*(top to bottom) Much of the Arctic is a cold desert called **tundra**. The coast of the Western Cordillera has a rain forest with huge trees. The Great Plains, or **prairies**, has flat land ideal for farming. **Hoodoos** are tall, thin structures of worn rock found in the Alberta badlands of the Great Plains.*

is for **seas**. Canada's motto "from sea to sea" should really be "from sea to sea to sea!" The country is bordered by oceans on three sides—the Pacific Ocean on the west, the Atlantic Ocean on the east, and the Arctic Ocean in the north. As a result, Canada has the longest coastline in the world! Canada also has more freshwater lakes than any other country.

*(top) Much of the east coast of Canada has majestic, rocky cliffs. (right) Some Canadian lakes are glacial lakes. These were formed thousands of years ago when huge sheets of ice called **glaciers** melted into valleys. (below) The Mackenzie Delta in the Northwest Territories has many small islands.*

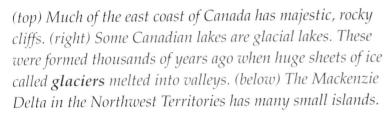

T is for **transportation**. Canada is a huge country, and Canadians use many types of transportation to get around and to move goods from place to place. Cars and trucks are the most common means of transportation. Other types of transportation include trains and airplanes. Canada's waterways, such as the large St. Lawrence Seaway, move bulky goods in large freight ships. In towns and cities, **public transit** such as buses and subways take people where they need to go.

Air Canada is a Canadian airline. Streetcars run along rails in the cities. Bombardier, a Canadian company, invented the snowmobile, which is a motorized sled.

U is for **Underground Railroad**. The Underground Railroad was not a railroad at all! It was a secret network of people who helped runaway slaves escape from the United States to Canada, where slavery was not allowed. Members of the Underground Railroad were called **conductors**. They offered runaway slaves a safe place to stay and helped them reach the next stop on their journey north. The Underground Railroad helped more than 40,000 slaves reach safety in Canada.

(right) Harriet Tubman is one of the most famous conductors of the Underground Railroad. From her home base in St. Catharines, Ontario, she helped more than 300 African Americans cross the border into Canada.

(below) Slaves on the run are heading for the Canadian border, where they will find safety and freedom.

is for **voyageurs**. *Voyageurs* is a French word meaning "travelers." The *voyageurs* were the traveling fur traders of Canada. When the fur trade boomed in the late 1600s, hundreds of European merchants and traders went to Canada hoping to get rich. Most settled around the St. Lawrence River. Over time, there were fewer beavers in this area, and trappers had to move farther inland to find furs. The *voyageurs* paddled along the St. Lawrence River and exchanged goods for the trappers' furs. They then traded the furs with the merchants for more goods. Over the years, these daring men explored and mapped most of North America's waterways.

Two voyageurs, *Pierre-Esprit Radisson and Médard des Groseilliers, traveled to Hudson Bay and discovered a wealth of beavers. They convinced British merchants to start a company to trade these furs. The Hudson's Bay Company, formed in 1684, is the oldest company in the world.*

W is for **wildlife**. Canada's many regions are home to a wide variety of wildlife. Canadian wildlife ranges from tiny mosquitoes to enormous whales that live in the oceans surrounding Canada. In the North, Arctic animals have plenty of space in which to live and hunt. In the southern part of Canada, however, animals are constantly losing their natural habitats to roads, homes, shopping centers, and other human developments. It is not uncommon for people to spot confused deer, bears, and mountain lions in their back yard! Some species of animals that have lost their habitats are **endangered**, or in danger of dying out. The peregrine falcon, sea otter, right whale, and wood bison are among Canada's endangered species.

(top) The Canada goose is a common bird. Every autumn, thousands of Canada geese fly south to escape the cold winter. They return in the spring.

(above) A male moose's antlers begin to grow in April and are shed every winter.

(left) Bears hunt for salmon and other fish in Canada's rivers.

XY are for **Xmas**, New **Year**, and other **yearly** holidays (see chart below). The Christmas season in Canada involves parades, gifts, Santa Claus, and Christmas trees. Many people spend Christmas Day with family and friends. Some families attend a church service on Christmas Eve or Christmas morning. Schools and most businesses remain closed on Boxing Day, the day after Christmas. Celebrations continue into the following week, when Canadians ring in the New Year at midnight on December 31. In February, Quebec is home to the world-famous winter carnival, *Carnaval d'Hiver*, shown in the picture below.

February	St. Valentine's Day, Carnaval d'Hiver
March	St. Patrick's Day
April	Passover, Easter
May	Mother's Day, Victoria Day
June	Father's Day, Quebec National Day
July	Canada Day
August	Civic Holiday
September	Labour Day
Sept./Oct.	Rosh Hashanah, Yom Kippur
October	Thanksgiving Day
November	Remembrance Day
December	Xmas, Hannukah, Kwanzaa

Bonhomme is the main character of the Quebec Winter Carnival.

is for **zones**—time zones, that is. The world is divided into 24 time zones, one for each hour of the day. Around the world from west to east, each time zone is one hour ahead of the one behind it. The idea of dividing the world into 24 time zones was invented in 1879 by a Canadian named Sir Sanford Fleming. Before he suggested time zones, every town on Earth set its own time according to the position of the sun. Canada is so huge that it covers six time zones. When Canadians in Vancouver are waking up, it is already past noon in Newfoundland! The clocks below show the time zones and an example of a Canadian city that falls in each one.

| *Pacific* | *Mountain* | *Central* | *Eastern* | *Atlantic* | *Newfoundland* |
| Vancouver | Calgary | Winnipeg | Toronto | Halifax | St. John's |

Words to know

area A measurement of land size

Calgary Stampede Calgary's large annual outdoor rodeo and fair

canal A narrow, human-made waterway that connects two bodies of water

capital The city in which a country, province, or territory's government is located

climate An area's typical long-term weather conditions

colony A territory ruled by another country

confederation The act of forming a union of provinces

entrepreneurs People who own and operate their own business

First Nations The first known groups of people to live in North America

multicultural Describing a society that includes many cultures

natural resources Things made by nature that are useful to people

parochial school A school that is supported by a church

Prime Minister The title for the leader of Canada

voyageurs French explorers and fur traders who traveled through North America in the 1600s

Index

1 2 3 4 5 6 7 8 9 0 Printed in the U.S.A. 8 7 6 5 4 3 2 1 0 9